CW00502597

Expressed Emotions:

Inspired by Life

DYAN N. CONSTANTINE

Self-Published

Copyright© 2023

Dyan N. Constantine

All rights reserved

The thoughts expressed in this body
of work are mine, inspired by my
thoughts, experiences, conversations,
and life in general.

ISBN: 9798360910039

Printed in the United States of
America

Cheers 🥂 to my loved ones, to my readers and supporters and the ones who will take pleasure in familiarizing themselves with my art.

Preface

Though my heart and my mind oftentimes work together, there are moments when they do not even agree on the simplest things.

Luckily for this book, my hands mediated, and they both came together making this production possible.

Where did the inspiration come from? Life. I see, hear, and even say things sometimes that become conversation pieces; I also have experienced many things which all this time were caged

in my mind and my heart – now I
release them to YOU.

Contents

I am a Woman

This finger, never wed

These breasts have never fed

However, I have bled

I am a woman

I am woman because God says so

Not woman because a court appointed
it

A woman with all the anatomy of one

I am a woman

In Motherhood, I chose not to reside

Taking care of an adult child, not for
me

A nurtured career is where I choose to be

I am a woman

Society's blueprint I do not fit

Those section lines my life contradicts

Though I am berated and abased

The fact remains, I am a woman

I Prayed My Way Out

I prayed my way out of depression

I prayed my way out of brokenness

I had to pray my way out toxicity

Prayer was needed to release me from it all

I prayed my way out of lacking

Went on my knees for deliverance from there

Through prayer and supplication, I gave it up

I prayed my way out of spiritual attacks

I prayed my way out of sinful desires

I cleared my thoughts through prayer

I prayed my way out of hurtful places

I asked Father Elohim to intervene on my behalf

I prayed my way out of mental illness

I prayed my way out of disrespect

I prayed my way out of being defensive

God answered my prayers and saw me out

Mom, Where Are You

I sure miss my mom

I look over and the person sitting
there looks like my mom

When she speaks, I recognize her
voice

but she is not the person I have loved
since birth The strong woman who
raised four children

Hustling to make sure there was a
roof over our heads and food on the
table

She was vibrant, with an unmatched
sense of humor

She could make any top chef feel
intimidated

She loved music, enjoyed old hits
parties

Recognized and cared for her grandchildren

Went for long walks with the aim to stay fit

Saturday mornings were her usual market days

But now, she struggles in her mind

Struggle to remember simple instructions

She finds it hard to put full, sensible sentence together

She packs, unpacks, and repacks her belongings

Always getting ready to go "home" while she is at home

A house she has been living for four years

It breaks my heart to see her like this

This has to be the worst disease
inflicted on people

As I observe her mental faculties slip
away every day

I get sadder as the days go by

I wish I could have one more day with
her as she was five or ten years ago.

I miss her input as I told her how my
day was

Mom, where are you?

Death is Lonely

Though many have gone on

the mystery still persists

Each had their own peace offering

Those who are en route cannot

explain to anyone what the trip is like

Death is indeed lonely, inexplicable
even

The grim reaper comes to each

as a berobed skeleton wielding a
scythe

Who he chooses, remains a mystery

When he does is oftentimes
unpredictable

Very lonely is death that it leaves
more

questions unanswered

Death is lonely

Life infinitely goes on

In its midst, Death is always present

Present but with no presence till it
happens

Marked for Death?

Yes, but without conviction

So, we go on without expecting its
arrival

Neither are we prepared

Nonetheless, Death is lonely

No return, no update, no perspective

The reality is, Death is lonely

Expressed Emotions

Only Slaves

Only slaves react only to authority

Only slaves require validation from
those at the apex

Only slaves act enslaved

Slaves do not know the difference
between being utilized and being used

Slaves operate from a place of praise

You know slaves by the way they act
with power

Condescending house slaves
subscribe to doctrines

they do not know nor understand

Only slaves grin and bear it instead of
articulating the source of their grouse

Only slaves are driven by money in
all instances

Only slaves are unaware that they are slaves

I Respect Your Response

May I be favoured with humility

To recognize that my journey

In this borrowed life is not mine

It is Yours and I am merely part of the
cast

I shall always respect your response

At times, it will be an outright yes

Sometimes, it will be not yet

There will be times when it will be no

That I know is fine with my soul

May I never become frustrated
spiritually

Nor curse at You in my thoughts

I pray that I will be gracious in all

My dealings with You

Be it prayer, fasting or worship

My heart's desire is to always

Respect Your Response

The Fallacy Called Friendship

You have a friend,

Who has a friend,

Who is not your friend

Secrets remain unsafe,

Stories are always told

A favour is asked,

A favour is given,

It is told without you knowing

Strangers look on with inexplicable
stares

You have rented space in their heads
for lengths unknown

Your friend, yes, your friend

Has caused this to happen to you

The unfriendly actions of a friendly human

Remains more dangerous than lewisite.

The Pressures of Life

"The pressures of life," she said
Immediately, I knew she was lying
Even though she was crying
My heart was unmoved

You may be feeling the pressures of
life
But that is not the reason
The decisions you have made are
more to blame
Your inability to love even yourself is
the "why"

Jacob was chastised for loving one
child more

God despises you for loving one and
hating the other
You may be a parent, but you are not
a mother
Honour you will not be served as you
are not deserving

All of life's pressures you now
experience
You have created out of hate
Borne out of your own need to be the
nucleus
The center of chaos and anarchy

Now you are alone
With your thoughts and memories
Your successes and failures

The missed opportunities to do good

How pressured life must feel to you

Life's pressures are not upon you

It is the pressure you have applied to

life

Which now comes to sit with you.

Preach and Practice

She preaches what she does not
practice

Her inability to do as she says

Makes it hard to respect her

Christian, says she is, but that is not
evident

Her relatives are always right

But it depends on whether with her,
they are all right

Justice, she knows not what that is

But she is inclined to wish evil for
others, a naysayer

Her need to be the apex of every
circle

Makes it impossible to realize her
ignorance

She boldly speaks rubbish and
gibberish

Hoping that a receptacle will accept it

As she ages, she becomes even worst

Disgusting to the point of disdain

Still hateful, bashful, and unforgiving

Pretending still, to those who like a
show

...she does not practice what she
preaches

I Am

I am rich in God's favour

I am rich in gratitude

I am healthy

I am faithful

I am intelligently quotient and
emotionally

I am beautiful

I am gracious

I am distinctly filled with purpose

I am intentionally kind

I am poised with promise

I am blessed in all I do

I am divinely curated

I am a success story

I am who Father Elohim says I Am

Expressed Emotions

I am chosen

We All Will Die Leaving It All

Hurry, hurry, hurry, to where?

Rush, rush, rush, for what?

Fight, fight, fight, who?

Where, what, who, why?

Where? Places where Yah has
removed His favour

What? Material things, those we can
never take back

Who? Anyone who seems to threaten
our need to grab

Why? Because we believe we are
immortal beings

No, we are not immortal beings

Nothing we have on earth will go with
us

Our energy is to be used to love not to
fight

Yah has said it, from dust we came

We will all die leaving it all

The houses, the cars, the clothes, the
shoes

Death is inevitable, it must be

Why not live happily, with wisdom,
and be free?

Jamaica Interdependence

Independent Jamaica is 60 in 2022

But she looks eighty-five

Her bank account is in the orange

And her underarms are green

The colours that once represented her

Have diminished in significance as
the black has been bleached

The gold has been stolen

And the green has been replaced by
concrete.

I cannot say happy independence to
her because she is not happy

I cannot say all the best to her because she is still in a relationship with politicians who rape her repeatedly

I cannot say things will get better because there is no evidence of that after so many years

But I will celebrate with her

Because despite all the negatives

Her eggs have produced some magnificent people.

The Enemy

Did you lock the gate?

Did you lock the grill?

Are the doors locked?

Is the bedroom door locked?

Who are you locking out?

What are you locking out?

Why all these safety needs?

…when the enemy is you?

You are your own enemy

You make the decisions that bring
you harm

You invite the demons to your circle

You unwisely trust the wrong people

The enemy will never be locked out

Can never be blocked out

The enemy is like a shadow

It can leave you in darkness but not in
the light

Are you your own enemy?

Think about these things

As that is what life brings

Wake up and see yourself – have a
mirror moment

Bathe Me

Bathe me in your prayers

So that I will enjoy the gifts of such a
bath

Bless me with your consecrated rag

For then I know I will be clean

Saturate my spirit with your divine
presence

Make my soul yearn for Thee

Massage my tongue with olives

That it may speak the language of
angels

Bless my heart's desires

So that they may fulfill my purpose

The same purpose you bathe me in

When you created a perfect specimen

Soak my soul in green pastures

That it may never want

Fight the very battles which were set
out to harm me

I ask Oh Lord to bathe me in your
garment

Tired

I am tired of being made to feel stupid

Tired of feeling dumb

Tired of you believing that I should think like you

Tired of being gaslighted

Tired of your micromanagement as if I am inept or incompetent

Tired of your paranoia which heightens my anxiety

Tired of holding my tongue as light as it is

Tired of having a grin when I really should not

Exhausted by your presence

Exasperated by your bombardment of my psyche

Perturbed by your menacing voice

Tired of your constant disruptions

Tired of your many requests

Tired of your horizontal priority list

Disgusted by your lack of a
conscience

Peeved by your lack of respect for my
ability

Sick and tired of you

...all of you

Robbed of my Freedom

Freedom to choose

Freedom to live

Freedom to sleep

Freedom to be free

My Freedom has been burglarized

I have the will, but My Freedom is
paralyzed

Breached by selfishness and
ingratitude

Assaulted by disregard and
disloyalty

Freedom to choose...

To dream

To eat

To stay or to go

Freedom to live...

In peace

In anarchy

Even in disquiet

Freedom to sleep...

Late

Naked

With the door unlocked

Freedom to be free...

Of guilt

Of burden

Of consideration

The Leading Lady

Who is the leading lady?

Of what?

Your life!

Where?

On earth

Who is the leading lady?

I am the leading lady of my life

I make the best decisions for me

I take front and center

Who is the leading lady?

It is she, who leads the charge

She, who fans the flame

She, whose focus is always on her

Who is the leading lady?

Do you mean that confident one with melanin?

The one who is not afraid to speak her truth?

Oh, do you mean the one who they love to hate?

Allow me to introduce myself to you

I am the leading lady!

The one and only

Leading lady of my life

Stressed Unnecessarily

We stress ourselves daily

Our goals are our priority

Time is used to worry

Berating others for their differences

Yet we will leave it all

We will leave it all

All the good

All the bad

All the in-between

Along the highways and byways

So many before us have left it all

Yet we take no lessons

We are inclined to believe we are
different

Our outcomes will be different

Then we leave it all

We leave it all

To the ungrateful

To the needy

To the greedy

To those who will leave it all...also

The Root Cause Analysis Anger

Analytically the root cause of this
anger

Has always been with me

In fact, I am somewhat a product of it

She broke me and continues to break
me

The root cause is the route cause

It holds the triggers and reactions

Unfortunately, it is a fight I must win

Fight to control me

I project it on every unrelated
situation and person

It roars its ugly head always

The suppression cup is full and
running over

I must confront this head-on

Would she admit it ever?

I doubt it and I suppose she will never

Knowing her, she too might be
projecting

Acting all perfect and righteous, me
never protecting

Unbelievably, her presence is
intolerable

I holler, sometimes inconsolable

Yet, I wish her well from afar

As my heart is not capable wage a
war

Sometimes it is the Mind

Sometimes it is the mind...

Which needs quieting

Which leads us foolishly

Which lies to us

Which haunts us

Sometimes it is the mind...

Where it all starts

Where peace is not present

Where our health begins to deteriorate

Where love or hate wins

Sometimes it is the mind...

Why we are stressed

Why we are depressed

Why we are owing

Why we do not know

Sometimes it is the mind

That takes us to places we have not
been

That sets us up to win

That coordinates our next decision

That gives us the ability to think

Sometimes it is in the mind where
many journeys begin and end.

Broken Womb

So many times, you have blossomed

Just as many times have you released
them

Your roots are watered

Where is the fruit?

You purge yourself each month

From there you prepare to be
fertilized

Nature travels to meet your roots

Sometimes you dismiss it before it
reaches

What do you need to be able to work?

How does one fix you?

Are you ordained to not bear fruit

Were you fractured from birth?

Each time you release the fruit before it is fit

It breaks many hearts, not only mine

I suffer in silence as each time it is personal

You make me so happy each time you bloom

Then you take me to a place which is darkly red

And it causes long-term grief and sorrow

No matter how time passes

May you one day be unbroken.

Heart Work

Matters of the heart require work,
heart work

Work on yourself and be honest about
it

To thine self be true, no matter what
is accrued

Above all else, guard your heart,

For everything you do flows from it

Proverbs 4:23

When the heart speaks, it is silently
loud

It incorporates all other organs

And like a piano, it plays on every
string

Create in me a clean heart, O God.

And renew the right spirit within me.

Psalm 51:10

Love comes naturally from the heart

But it can be hindered by hate

Hate creates envy and animosity

It borrows nothing from God

Thou shalt not hate thy brother in thine heart

Leviticus 19:17

Be of good courage, and he shall strengthen your heart, all ye that hope in the Lord.

Psalm 31:24

Memory

I wake each day with a vague memory

Memory is fleeting

I see a picture of me

Yet I see someone else

I stare at the television

With no recall of what was said one
minute ago

Where has my memory gone?

They ask me questions

I just do not know the answers to

My children in sequential order

I do not remember

It stresses me, no matter the
reassurance

I am alive, but am I living?

Where has my memory gone?

They say once a man, twice a child

My childhood though, I have no
memory of

Hallucination has replaced my reality

Silence has become my new normal

If only my brain would not talk so
much

It scares me each time

Where has my memory gone?

Where has my memory gone?

Why has it eluded me?

Why has my memory gone AWOL?

It must have grown tired of the
traumas

Perhaps it too could not stand the
anger of my heart

I am sorry, not just for you, but for us

Where has my memory gone?

I Dream of Raising a King

We are living in Queensland
We have so many Kingdoms
Ruled by Queens
We need some Kings

I want to raise a King!
There are far too many Peasant-
Pleasers
Parading Castles as Kings
Chauvinistic goons profiling as Kings

Yah, give me a seed that will
Blossom and bloom majestically
One which will operate in the divine
A soul which sees himself as a King

I dream of raising a King

One who will attract the favour of
Yah always

Kingdom-bound activities will be his

I will nurture this king till he becomes
a King!

Does God Leave Voids?

Some say they hear from Him

Others blindly believe

Others believe what Others tell them
to

Some continue to search in earnest

Then there are those who

Do not believe

Cannot believe

Shocked out of belief

Search for answers elsewhere

The question is

Does God leave a void?

The lack of direct, tangible contact

The lack of answers

The lack of evidence

The need for a morse code translator

Does the mystery of God cause

People to seek out sorcerers

Become witches

Practice voodoo

Become an outright atheist?

Does a void, if it exists, justify these things?

Towns

Born downtown

Sometimes shop uptown

Midtown is a playground

Feeling for some fish?

Check Ratty in Rae Town

Franklyn Town, I know not but
Rollington Town I have been

My innocence went in Vineyard
Town

My mother's roots are in Trench
Town

West Kingston has the most towns

Albert Town, Hannah Town just to
name a few

Spent five years toiling in Allman
Town

Abuse forced a stay in August Town

Expressed Emotions

#Hashtag

#Ninemonths

#SingleMother

#NoFather

#ThreeSiblings

#Poor

#Struggle

#Angry

#Abusive

#Frustration

#Loss

#Faith #Belief

#Deliverance

#Admiration

#ShiningExample

#Tenement

#Garrison

#Education

#Hunger

#Love

#Malice

#Jealousy

#Change

#Honesty

#Abundance

#Testament

#Tesimony

Las Palabras

Conoce las palabras

Conoce su impacto

Comprende la diferencia

Es importante para la vida, no sólo

para el servicio al cliente

Las palabras pueden ser positivas

Las palabras pueden ser negativas

Las palabras pueden ser neutrales

Las palabras positivas como sí, yo, yo

lo haré y desde luego, dan confianza y

muestran carácter,

Las palabras negativas como no, ellos,

no puedo y no lo sé causan enojo y

muestran que uno es irresponsable

Las palabras neutras como nosotros,

lo intentaré y no estoy seguro, pero;

muestran que hay responsabilidad,

compromiso y apoyo

La lengua es ligera, pero puede causar

un daño mayor a las relaciones, tanto

personales como en los negocios

Sean prudentes y considerados en su

uso

También, piensen antes de hablar

Married Yet Separated

We sleep on separate beds in the same
room

We sleep in separate rooms in the
same house

We sleep in separate houses in the
same community

The community believes we are
together

Our children know we are apart

We have no desire to stay with each
other

Yet we feign a loving lifestyle one to
another

Why did we get married?

I was pregnant

I was in the church

I was never going to abort it

I had to legitimize the fornication

Why did we get married?

Fornication resulted in a conception

My position in the church

My job says I must

Why did we get married?

She tricked me with a fake pregnancy

Her job required it

She said all her girlfriends were
married

It is what our parents wanted

Raised Poor, not Poorly

One thing is certain

Two things for sure, yes, I flipped it

I was raised poor

But I was never raised poorly

Verily, Verily I say onto you

My mother instilled some good values and

Principles of Life in me

The Potter potted a good pot

A mold was made and is now broken

The farmer took care of this farm

My upbringing was carefully minted

Not dragged like a vulture hauling a carcass

Abject poverty did not subject me to being an object or subject of Poverty

I was not raised poorly, because my mother was not raised so, even though she too was raised poor.

Value System

My reality has been tarnished

I have no sense of right or wrong

Your imposed belief system has
rattled me

The constant bombardment of my
mind

Makes it impossible to utilize my
willpower

You exert your authority on my
decisions

You choose what is right at a time
convenient to you

Your propensity to hate makes it
impossible to be fair

The words in your vocabulary
constantly war with each other as you
lack principle…

The principle to not be duplicitous

The principle of not being biased in judgment

You value those who do not reciprocate

Mistreat those who would go to battle for you

Help me to fix it I ask of Thee

Helel's Interference

Yah knows what He made

He also knows what has been

interfered with

Yah does not make mistakes

His perfection goes beyond our mortal

understanding

Yet Helel positions himself to impede

Yah's goals

Helel continues to interfere with

Yah's intention for His people

Our disobedience allows him to be

successful in his attempts

Our spirit yields to sin and Helel is

aware of that weakness

Joshua 1:9 reminds us

But we are still persuaded to be weak
and fearful
Helel will continue to interfere if we
present an atmosphere conducive to
his games.

1 Timothy 6:10

Your love for money is unattractive

It borderlines ungodliness

You have defiled yourself for the love of it

Spilled innocent blood for the love of it

Your family has suffered due to your affinity for money

You have neglected your responsibilities due to this unhealthy love affair

Immorality has created a destructive path for you because of your love for money

Without admission, there can be no correction

Check yourself before regret is your
only emotion

No Bounds

Your arrogance knows no bounds
Your hatred knows no bounds
Your dishonesty knows no bounds
Your disloyalty knows no bounds

Your love knows no bounds
Your peace knows no bounds
Your promise knows no bounds
Your commitment knows no bounds

You are bound to sin
You are bound to transgressions
You are bound to this world
You are bound to death

Your forgiveness knows no bounds

Your words have no bounds

Your miracles have no bounds

Your praises have no bounds

…that is why I and my household
shall forever have no bounds in
worshipping You

Hostage to the Past

Why are you bound by the past?

Are you afraid to detach?

Will you die if you let go?

Have you ever tried to free yourself?

You hold yourself captive to
intangible chains

You impose barriers on your abilities

Imprisoned by your thoughts of
events gone

Paranoid by what-ifs and negative
scenarios

While the past is dead, gone,
forgotten

You continuously live in its shadows

Marking yourself as a victim

Imposing imaginary boundaries

Pass the past

Give your mind a spring clean,

Adjust the sails

…enter your future by being present

It is Always Enough

It is always enough

Your provisions know no limit

Though it gets rough

It is always enough

Enough to fill me up

Enough to fill my cup

It is always enough

Your security and sincerity

Your prosperity and tenacity

It is always enough

Your ability to forgive

Your decision to not hold us to
scrutiny

It is always enough

Though we lack the ability to serve
you

Your commitment and promise to us

Is always enough

May your grace and favour be always
enough

To remind us that being enough
requires effort

Efforts in our fasting

Effort in our sacrifices

Efforts in our fellowship

Efforts in our praying

Because these are always enough for
Yah.

I am not Submissive

You do not see yourself as a King

Why should I treat you like one?

You were raised to impress minions

Your upbringing dictates that peasants
are to be pleased

Yet you want to be treated like a King

Do you want me to submit to you?

Where is your crown?

Where is your true belief in self?

Did you come from a submissive
woman?

Was your father a King in your eyes?

Do you know what Kings do?

Do you possess the penchant of a
King?

Come on now, dust yourself off

There is room for growth and an
unoccupied throne

Take yourself in arms and gather your
tools

Much work is required in that mind of
yours

Do not be dismayed, I want to submit

I only will do so to a true King

Not one which seeks the admiration
of crofters

No, not one who seeks validation
from sycophants

One who is valiant in his effort to
command my respect

One who will respect himself enough

To not lower his standard to fit in

Allow me the opportunity to be
submissive

Praying Preys

Some who pray are preying
There is no praise in preying
Predatory monitoring spirits
Lurking in the wings
Camouflaged in pretense, these
carnivores devour prosperity
Careful of those who lay hands on
you, they oftentimes project undivine
spirits on one's soul
Do not entertain all those who
sympathize and empathize
Some are not praying with you; they
are preying on you and yours

Their prayers though, will not
manifest that which resides in their
hearts.

Dem

How do Jamaicans generally pluralize
words?...

Right now, mi foot dem tired

But mi still a go a di people dem work

Mi friend dem seh dem waah go Ochi

But my two card dem empty

Di pickney dem loud like a sound
system

Di teacha dem muss tiad a dem

Even dem parents a dem yaad must
frustrated wid dem

Dem nuh listen to adults

Dem politician yah nuh have nuh
heart

Dem sell out di country to dem friend
dem

Mi nuh go a dem place deh, dem too expensive

Dem gwaan like seh a dem alone fi live!

Prayer of Release!

Burst up that ground that has held us
down
Wash away those trenches which have
us on benches
Make our way clear of all paganist
peddlers
Remove those who seek the services
of sorcerers
Sink ships that bring loads of
depression
Disband those who pray bad prayers
even though to them there will be no
answers
Rescue us from the battlefield of
powers and principalities of darkness

Gratitude

My arms are parallel in unison to the
sky

Sometimes I am crying,

Sometimes I am smiling

This motion without speech depicts
my gratitude

Gratitude for all things

Those I did not ask for

Those I prayed for, and

Those I have no clue of

Grateful for life

So, I do not complain

Grow wherever I am planted because
my journey is not my own

Working on my heart for it need not
be affected by the things of this world

Of the grand awareness that I am not immortal and for that I must tap into a source to regain my strength, renew my commitment, and give praise

...and so, it ends...

Expressed Emotions

Reading is fulfilling, join a library or visit the bookstore.

Thank you

Asante

Gracias

Merci

Grazie

Contact
the
Author

Email: fatherlessdaughter3@gmail.com
Instagram: authoredbydy

Printed in Great Britain
by Amazon

15830842R10061